Orla Wade

Antoni Gaudí and Friedensreich Hundertwasser

DATE DUE FOR RETURN

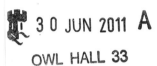

D1333932

The loan period may be shortened if the item is requested.

Orla Wade

Antoni Gaudí and Friedensreich Hundertwasser

Imagination and creativity, similarities in architectural style

VDM Verlag Dr. Müller

Impressum/Imprint (nur für Deutschland/ only for Germany)

Bibliografische Information der Deutschen Nationalbibliothek: Die Deutsche Nationalbibliothek verzeichnet diese Publikation in der Deutschen Nationalbibliografie; detaillierte bibliografische Daten sind im Internet über http://dnb.d-nb.de abrufbar.

Alle in diesem Buch genannten Marken und Produktnamen unterliegen warenzeichen-, marken- oder patentrechtlichem Schutz bzw. sind Warenzeichen oder eingetragene Warenzeichen der jeweiligen Inhaber. Die Wiedergabe von Marken, Produktnamen, Gebrauchsnamen, Handelsnamen, Warenbezeichnungen u.s.w. in diesem Werk berechtigt auch ohne besondere Kennzeichnung nicht zu der Annahme, dass solche Namen im Sinne der Warenzeichen- und Markenschutzgesetzgebung als frei zu betrachten wären und daher von jedermann benutzt werden dürften.

Coverbild: www.purestockx.com

Verlag: VDM Verlag Dr. Müller Aktiengesellschaft & Co. KG
Dudweiler Landstr. 99, 66123 Saarbrücken, Deutschland
Telefon +49 681 9100-698, Telefax +49 681 9100-988, Email: info@vdm-verlag.de
Zugl.:

Herstellung in Deutschland:
Schaltungsdienst Lange o.H.G., Berlin
Books on Demand GmbH, Norderstedt
Reha GmbH, Saarbrücken
Amazon Distribution GmbH, Leipzig
ISBN: 978-3-639-20793-4

1006431882

Imprint (only for USA, GB)

Bibliographic information published by the Deutsche Nationalbibliothek: The Deutsche Nationalbibliothek lists this publication in the Deutsche Nationalbibliografie; detailed bibliographic data are available in the Internet at http://dnb.d-nb.de .

Any brand names and product names mentioned in this book are subject to trademark, brand or patent protection and are trademarks or registered trademarks of their respective holders. The use of brand names, product names, common names, trade names, product descriptions etc. even without a particular marking in this works is in no way to be construed to mean that such names may be regarded as unrestricted in respect of trademark and brand protection legislation and could thus be used by anyone.

Cover image: www.purestockx.com

Publisher:
VDM Verlag Dr. Müller Aktiengesellschaft & Co. KG
Dudweiler Landstr. 99, 66123 Saarbrücken, Germany
Phone +49 681 9100-698, Fax +49 681 9100-988, Email: info@vdm-publishing.com

Printed in the U.S.A.
Printed in the U.K. by (see last page)
ISBN: 978-3-639-20793-4

Antoni Gaudi and Friedensreich Hundertwasser.

Imagination and creativity, similarities in architectural style.

Orla Wade

Acknowledgements

First and foremost, I would like to thank my parents, Annette and Michael, for always guiding me in the right direction and for their endless support. I could never have accomplished this without you. I would also like to express my sincere gratitude to my brother Kenneth, for his expert advice and invaluable guidance.

Table of Contents

Chapter Three: **Similarities between Gaudí's and Hundertwasser's works**

4

Introduction

Antoni Gaudí is not only a well renowned Spanish architect, painter and sculptor of the twentieth century, but one of the most applauded architects worldwide. The flamboyant Austrian architect Friedensreich Hundertwasser has also earned worldwide recognition and is respected as one of the world's greatest artists.

Both architects were innovators, but some of their works show amazing similarity. The purpose of this book is to provide an overview of each architect's life, examining the theories and ideologies which shaped their work and examine to what extent their works share similar elements.

Gaudi, who died in 1926, two years before the birth of Hundertwasser, was constantly exposed to nature as a boy. This was to have an enormous impact on his architectural work. Gaudí followed a gothic style and his preference was to use natural lines and basic raw materials in his constructions. He also liked to decorate surfaces with a multitude of colourful tiles, which is referred to as the *Aragonese trencadís* technique.[1] The majority of his buildings boast unique fabrication and an unwavering sense of colour and are some of the most important landmarks of Barcelona.

Hundertwasser, too, was a talented architect, sculptor and painter who preferred the realm of the senses and used fierce colours and natural lines to design his unusual creations. He was a firm believer in environmentalism and his most imaginative works are characterised by land, sea and sky. The main theme in his work is the rejection of straight lines:

"The horizontal line belongs to nature, the vertical to man".

---

[1] Antoni Gaudí: The complete buildings, Rainer Zerbst, Taschen, 2002 p.95

Having examined the lives and careers of both Gaudi and Hunderwasser, the book then examines similarities between some of their works. Hundertwasser himself revealed that his work was strongly influenced by the works of Antoni Gaudí:

"My building will have something of Gaudi"[2]

This can best be seen in the Hundertwasserhaus, the Rogner-Bad Blumau, Hotel and Spa and in the Church of St. Barbara, which are examined in chapter three of this book, and which reveal the main similarities between the works of the two men- in their use of vivid colours, tiling, the influence of nature, utilising inexpensive materials and natural shapes.

---

[2] Hundertwasser, Harry Rand, 1991 Benedikt Taschen, Verlag p.210

Chapter One- Antoni *Gaudí* (1852-1926)

"The most ingenious of all architects"[3]

1.1- An overview of Gaudí's life and career

Antoni Plácid Guillem Gaudí Cornet was born in Reus, Spain on June 25 1852. He was
the fifth and youngest son of a coppersmith. As a young boy he was fascinated by nature,
its shapes and colours. As a student he excelled at geometry, poetry and Greek. His
religious nature probably evolved from his schooling with the Escolapius Fathers.[4]
Gaudí suffered with rheumatism from the early age of five; this in turn limited his ability
to engage with other children. Due to considerable pain, he would ride a donkey when he
wanted to venture from his home; therefore he was continuously exposed to nature and its
design, which was to have a significant impact on his later artistic development and can
be seen in Gaudí's furniture, which expresses the structure of each piece in curving,
naturalistic forms which emphasise joints and connections and which are strongly
influenced by his early exposure and interest in nature.

Chair created for Casa Battló

---

[3] Antoni Gaudí i Cornet, A life dedicated to Architecture, Rainer Zerbst, 1993 Benedikt Taschen, Verlag P6
[4] http://www.furnituresociety.org/fin/*Gaudí*.html (18/12/2006)

Throughout his life, he was fascinated by nature and always incorporated it into his designs. He integrated hyperboloid structures, parabolic arches, organic shapes and fluidity of water into his architecture, which allowed his designs to resemble elements from the environment. He was inspired by nature and natural lines[5]

Parc Güell (1900-1914), Barcelona

In 1867, Gaudí published his first drawings in *El Arlequin* newspaper, which was distributed in handwritten copies in Reus.[6] The following year, Gaudí moved to Barcelona to study architecture at the *Escola Técnica Superior d'Arquitectura* and graduated in 1878. While in Barcelona, he assisted many builders, which in turn influenced his architectural style. Gaudí worked with an array of materials such as concrete, wrought iron, coloured glass, stone and faience. Faience is a Middle East invention of a pottery glaze suitable for painted decoration. During his studies he made drafts for a cemetery gate, a central hospital for Barcelona and a landing stage for ships. Shortly before finishing his studies, he was awarded with his first public contract. He was commissioned to design street lights for the city of Barcelona, the first of which were installed in 1879.

---

[5] http://0-find.galegroup.com.millennium.it-tallaght.ie/ips/retrieve.do?subjectParam=Lo... (16/10/2006)

[6] Antoni Gaudí i Cornet, A life dedicated to Architecture, Rainer Zerbst, 1993 Benedikt Taschen, Verlag P232

The writer Luis Gueilburt states how Gaudí's first successful commission was a piece of furniture. It was a display cabinet for the Spanish Pavilion at the Universal Exposition of 1878 in Paris[7]. During the Paris World Fair, in which Gaudí's projects were exhibited, he attracted the attention of a man whose personality was similar to that of the young architect, Count Eusebi Güell I Bacigalupi[8], a wealthy Catalan who became one of Gaudí's first patrons. The same year he was awarded the title of architect[9]. Gaudí's career was closely linked to the Güell family, a family with huge prestige in artistic and industrial circles at this time in Barcelona.

In 1884, Gaudí redesigned Güell's estate in Barcelona. He built the entrance way and stables for the Güell Estate in Les Corts.[10] Most importantly, he also built the magnificent Palau Güell in Barcelona-built between 1886 and 1889. This building, a family home, is truly a product of the imagination, with richly decorated odd looking chimneys. It also has an "underground car Park" for horse carriages. One of Gaudí's truly amazing creations is the Parc Güell, a municipal Park in Barcelona. Originally designed as a housing estate, only two houses were actually built. However, it is the work on the public areas of the Park which are truly spectacular. In addition, another of Gaudí's developments Colonia Güell, was sponsored by and dedicated to the Güell family. This assignment entailed a housing development for a small settlement of workers next to Eusebi Güell's textile factory in Santa Coloma but was never completed.[11]

[7] http://www.furnituresociety.org/fin/Gaudi.html (18/12/2006)
[8] Antoni Gaudí i Cornet, A life dedicated to Architecture, Rainer Zerbst, 1993 Benedikt Taschen, Verlag P25
[9] http://www.furnituresociety.org/fin/Gaudi.html (18/12/2006)

[10] Antoni Gaudí i Cornet, A life dedicated to Architecture, Rainer Zerbst, 1993 Benedikt Taschen, Verlag P233
[11]
thp0C&pg=PA121&lpg=PA121&ots=cEmVmVHVVx&dq=what+is+colonia+guell,+gaudi&sig=g4zo4nQ PdJKauR1gqqMBV7T6wYM#PPA123,M1 14/04/2007

Palau Güell(1886-1889)

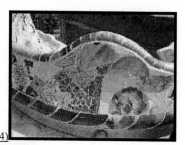

Parc Güell(1900-1914)

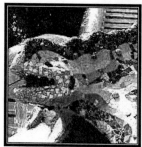

Lizard, Parc Güell(1900-1914)

Colonia Güell

In the early stage of his career, Gaudí created graduated distinctive work influenced by the Art Nouveau movement. Of particular importance, are his Art Nouveau inspired houses such as: Casa Vicens, Casa Battló and Casa Milá.

Casa Vicens (1883-1888)

Casa Battló(1904-1906)

<u>Casa Milá(1906-1910)</u>

In addition, Gaudí also designed a lot of furniture at this time. Most of the furniture that Gaudí designed for his patrons was lost during the Civil War. The remaining pieces of furniture form a private collection in Paris. In 1910, Gaudí refused other commissions and devoted his life to building the famous cathedral La Sagrada Família, perhaps his greatest achievement, which he started in 1883. Driven by his religious passion, Gaudí became obsessed with this work, eventually living on site. He poured his entire material and spiritual self into the work- which he was never to finish. On June 8, 1926, Gaudí was run over by a tram. Many cab drivers refused to pick him up because of his ragged look, for fear that he would be unable to pay for his fare. He was brought to a pauper's hospital in Barcelona Hospital de la Santa Creu, and when his friends tried to move him to a nicer hospital, he refused saying :

"I belong here among the poor"[12]

On 10 June, 1926, he was buried in the midst of his unfinished masterpiece La Sagrada Família, on which he had spent the majority of his life working. The Government instructed that he be laid to rest in the crypt and the Pope granted approval.[13]

Gaudí is considered one of Spain's most talented architects with a rich imagination and a willingness to embrace new styles. His works are rich in improvisation, mystery and

---

[12] http://www.furnituresociety.org/fin/*Gaudí*.html (18/12/2006)

[13] Antoni Gaudí i Cornet, A life dedicated to Architecture, Rainer Zerbst, 1993 Benedikt Taschen, Verlag P6

surprise. Many of his plans and designs were destroyed and lost during the Spanish Civil War, but 1952 marked the start of the Gaudí Renaissance.

Gaudí is noted as one of the most extraordinary designers of this century. He was a man with an unwavering sense of form and colour, a sculptor, who at the same time was a painter. He concentrated his efforts on Santander, León (the Bishops Palace in Astorga and Casa de los Botines) and of course on Barcelona. In 2006 he was proposed for beatification by the Archbishop of Barcelona.[14] His most famous works are among the most important tourist landmarks of Barcelona.

1.2- Gaudí's theories and ideologies

Gaudí initially followed a Gothic style but immersed himself completely into developing his own style. Apart from the occasional reference to *Art Nouveau*, all imitative elements disappeared from his work. He unwaveringly gave his architectonic fantasies full reign using pure figments of the imagination. One the most intriguing aspects of Gaudí's work are the mixture of materials he used in his buildings. He preferred to use everyday materials; he created veritable wonders out of the simplest materials. The mixture of ornamental-looking tiles and cheap stone is a reoccurring feature in his work.

The *Mudèjar* style of art, an art and architecture of Islamic derivation arising on the Iberian Peninsula in the eleventh century was revived in the nineteenth century and was incorporated into some of Gaudí's buildings.[15] The exteriors of Casa Vincens (1883-1888), El Capricho (1883-1885) and the Güell Pavilions (1884-1887) are thoroughly indicative of his interpretation of the *Mudèjar* style.

He often decorated surfaces with an array of colourful tiles, which is also referred to as the *Aragonese trencadís* technique. The use of tiles is clearly evident on the curved benches in Gaudí's *Parc Güell,* a Municipal Park in Barcelona. The spectacular gyres of mosaics suggest waves of sea and complement creativity and fairytale.

---

[14] Ibid (18/12/2006)
[15] Antoni Gaud Judith Carmel-Arthur, Carlton, 1999 P22

The Güell Parc Bench

 Many of Gaudí's arches in his buildings are designed upside down as he hung various weights on interconnected strings and used gravity to calculate catenaries for a natural curved arch. Gaudí also believed that nature is not monochromatic and if anyone praised the banal sand coloured stone used in the façade of La Sagrada Família, he usually reported *"It's going to be painted over"*.[16] He always introduced color into his facades. Improvising designs from odd bits of material, such as rubble, bricks, and polychrome tiles, he also achieved variegated effects, evoking comparisons to abstract expressionism and surrealism.

He departed further from the artificiality of building, and drew closer to nature. His affinity with nature clearly distinguishes him from other Art Nouveau artists. Art Nouveau is based on natural forms, but remains purely ornamental and two dimensional. For Gaudí, however, nature consisted of forces that work beneath the surface. He once asked a visitor in his workshop:

"Do you want to know where I found my model?", *"An upright tree; it bears its branches and these, in turn, their twigs, and these, in turn, the leave .And every individual growing*

---

[16] Antoni Gaudí i Cornet, A life dedicated to Architecture, Rainer Zerbst, 1993 Benedikt Taschen, Verlag P30

part has been growing harmoniously, magnificently, ever since God the artist created it".
[17]

His theory of belief in an upright tree is reflected in the construction of the pillars in the nave of La Sagrada Família, where the forest of pillars branch out and upward in many directions.

Gaudí's aspiration was to depart from conventional walls; his best structures are hollow spaces. At the crafts and trades fair in Munich in 1974, the prominent German architect Josef Wiedemann praised Gaudí's work:
"His structures are soothing oases in the wasteland of functional buildings, precious gems in the uniform grey lines of houses, creations pulsating with melodic rhythm in the dead mass of their surroundings".[18]

The Sagrada Familia is almost symbolic of this. Light and colour play an important role in Gaudí's buildings. The main tower, as Gaudí had planned, soaring up above all else and symbolizing Christ, was to be lit up by spotlights from the twelve "towers of the Apostles". Also, Gaudí intended to beam strong light from the cross- where the tower was meant to end- over the city to illustrate Christ's words *"I am the light".*[19]

Colours were used symbolically in his work. He found monotony of colour unnatural and gave all elements of architecture a touch of colour. In the Sagrada Familia Gaudí used monotonous colours in the Western Portal, portraying Christ's suffering. In contrast, he used green in the Portal of Hope.

---

[17] IbidP30
[18] IbidP34
[19] Ibid P201

1.3- Gaudí's influences

Gaudí studied the Neo-Gothic style. A French architect by the name of Eugene Viollet-le-Duc, who promoted gothic architecture, had a major influence on Gaudí.[20] He even travelled to Carcassone, where Viollet-le-Duc had restored the old section of the city.[21] Gaudí surpassed Villet-le-Duc and produced his own irregular and bold masterpieces. He was placed into a category of *sui generic* as a result of adopting biomorphic shapes rather than orthogonal lines[22].

He immersed himself completely in developing his own style and found inspiration in gothic style art and medieval books. His personal love for music also contributed to his original style. The person whose theories he adhered to the most was an English writer John Ruskin, who conveyed to Gaudí his belief that *"ornament is the origin of architecture".*[23] When Gaudí died in 1926, he left behind an unfinished opus, however he had no successors and his work could not be carried on. But Gaudí's style was later echoed by the works of the Austrian architect Friedensreich Hundertwasser (1928-2000).

1.4- Some of Gaudí's most popular works

One of the most astonishing facts about Gaudí is his utilisation of materials. The raw materials he preferred to use were of an inferior quality and thus less durable, so they posed great constructional problems. Despite this problem, his fascinating architectonic designs are successful and incomparable. Three of his most famous works will be discussed in this work-his unfinished cathedral, La Sagrada Família, the municipal Park, Parc Güell, and the apartment block the Casa Milá.

---

[20] http://en.wikipedia.org/wiki/Antoni_Gaud%C3%AD (18/12/2006)
[21] Antoni Gaudí i Cornet, A life dedicated to Architecture, Rainer Zerbst, 1993 Benedikt Taschen, Verlag P12
[22] Ibid (18/12/2006)

[23] http://studentwebs.coloradocollege.edu/~j_becker/biography.htm (18/12/2006)

La Sagrada Família (1883-1926) (The Sacred Family), in Barcelona has an almost hallucinatory power. On November 3 1883, Gaudí received the commission for the building from the architect Francisco de Paula de Villar.[24] The work of the stone structured cathedral began in 1884 and has been ongoing under the auspices of the Sagrada Família Foundation. The east transept with four 100metre towers was completed during Gaudí's lifetime.

Between the years of 1884 and 1887, the crypt was built and by 1900 the eastern façade "The façade of the Nativity" was completed. Funding was based on donations, which, in return delayed the construction of the church. In 1886, Gaudí still believed he would complete the Sagrada Familia in as little as ten years as long as he received 360,000 pesetas per year. By 1918, Gaudí's final design for the "Façade of the Passion" (the western side), which took thirty years to construct, was completed. This façade, where the sun goes down, was devoted to the sufferings of Christ in Gaudí's plans.[25]

In the final years of his life, Gaudí lived in his small workshop on the site. One year after Gaudí's death, work on the three bell towers at the eastern façade commenced. Unfortunately in 1936, there was a fire in the crypt and some of Gaudí's archives with drawings and models were partially destroyed.[26] Moreover, further damage to the site took place during the civil war. In 1954, the foundations for the western façade were laid and in remembrance of the fiftieth anniversary of Gaudí's death, in 1976, the spires on the western façade were completed. The overall model envisaged twelve bell-towers, four for each façade, which are a main symbol and a landmark for Barcelona as a whole. Each tower is dedicated to an apostle. Gaudí placed a crowning boss on each tower, which from a distance has the appearance of a bishop's mitre.[27] Gaudí imagined the church as the body of Christ and the centre of Christ is represented by the altar inside the church.[28]

---

[24] http://www.cbrava.com/Gaudi.uk.htm (18/12/2006)
[25] Antoni Gaudí i Cornet, A life dedicated to Architecture, Rainer Zerbst, 1993 Benedikt Taschen, Verlag P200
[26] Ibid P235
[27] Ibid P198
[28] Ibid

La Sagrada Família has being worked on for more than one century, interpreting architectural models Gaudí prepared in his final years.[29] The high arches are repeated in the design of the slender soaring towers. The spires of the four towers on the façade devoted to Christ reveal the use of loud colours characteristic of Parc Güell. It is probably impossible to find a church building anything like this in the entire history of art. As the writer Roger Hughes states in his book, *The Shock of the New,*
"This is the last imperious monument of Catholic Spain".[30]

La Sagrada Família (1883-1926)

---

[29] http://0-find.galegroup.com.millennium.it-tallaght.ie/ips/retrieve.do?subjectParam=Lo... (16/10/2006)
[30] Antoni Gaudí,Judith Carmel-Arthur,Carlton, 1999 P13

Parc Güell (1900-1914) –Architect and Count Eusebi Güell, Gaudí's most ardent admirer and sponsor was quite impressed with the English landscape gardens and wanted Gaudí to create something similar in Barcelona. Gaudí was to create a garden-city in harmony with the countryside, but only two of the buildings originally planned for Parc Güell were built.[31] With this project, Gaudí put his comprehensive concept of the architect's profession into practice for the first time. Architecture and nature enter a unique alliance in the Parc Güell project. It reveals the overflowing imagination of an architect quite drunk with colours. It was built with the cheapest of raw materials, most of which were found on the actual site.[32] The eye encounters a wealth of bright, garish colours, enriching the beauty and individuality of the Park. Gaudí adorned all the features of the Park with strong colours, such as the endlessly long bench, decorated with ceramic tiles which run through the Park in the form of a snake. This surface design is perhaps the most opulent and artistic utilization of "broken ceramics".

The entrance area of the Park points to the main constructions in the Park: dumbfounding effects of gleaming materials that attract the eye as if by magic. Gaudí created an abundance of organic sculptors, stairs, bright scales, and symbolic creations. As always, in the case of Gaudí's work, there is symbolic meaning lurking behind what appears to be playful on the surface. The dragon represents Python, guardian of the subterranean waters. Behind the dragon there's a cistern that contains 2,600 gallons of water, to irrigate the barren Parkland. A snake's head also serves as an overflow valve for the cistern. The outside columns are true to Greek custom and also hold great significance. The hallow columns are not just pillars supporting a roof; they serve as a drainage system for rainwater. The roof serves as a "market place". The whole Park as it was originally planned could be seen as one large amphitheatre. In 1906, the "Garden Party" for the first Congress of the Catalan language was held there.[33] When Eusebi Güell died, his heirs decided they did not want the responsibility of such a gigantic urban project and offered it for sale to the City Hall in 1922. The site was purchased and converted into a

---

[31] Antoni Gaudí i Cornet, A life dedicated to Architecture, Rainer Zerbst, 1993 Benedikt Taschen, Verlag P27
[32] Antoni Gaudí i Cornet, A life dedicated to Architecture, Rainer Zerbst, 1993 Benedikt Taschen, Verlag P148
[33] Gaudí of Barcelona, Lluís Permanyer, Barcelona 1997 P108

building built / used / transformed.

municipal Park in 1923. It was declared an artistic monument by the Barcelona civic authorities in 1926 and by 1969, the Spanish Government declared it a national monument.[34]

In 1984 the Park was placed under an international preservation order by UNESCO.[35] Today, there is a museum which displays furniture from Casa Battló and Casa Calvet in the Park. Eusebi Güell had intended the Park to be anything but a private residential estate. He had planned an exemplary suburban colony, a paradise of homes, and a town of gardens. Yet, a Park is what emerged- to the benefit of all Barcelona.

+ PP 140 used.

Parc Güell

---

[34] Ibid P112
[35] Antoni Gaudí i Cornet, A life dedicated to Architecture, Rainer Zerbst, 1993 Benedikt Taschen, Verlag P161

Casa Milá (1906-1910) this apartment block is also known as *"La Pedrera"*, the Catalan for quarry. The colour and the surface of the house are actually reminiscent of a quarry. This is Gaudí's largest apartment house project. [36] The house has the character of a detached building and the roof sports an imitation of the bench in Parc Güell and a humorous landscape of almost surreal sculptors, which serve as chimneys and air ducts. Nothing is uniform and the ground plans for each floor are completely different to each other.

The rooms are all of different heights in keeping with the wavy façade. The furniture that he created for the house was unmistakably fashioned after the human body. Moreover, the staircase of the house reflects the same shape as the backbone of a dinosaur.[37] The door handles were shaped in such a way that they could be taken for bones. He incorporated a lot of religious symbols into his buildings and had planned to mount a series of dedications to the Virgin Mary on the façade. During the construction of Casa Milá, there was an uprising of clergymen in Barcelona, also known as "Semana Trágica" in 1909. As a result of this, the owner of the building rejected the idea to adorn the building with a series of religious representations.[38] Therefore, Gaudí was unable to gain acceptance for his views and the detailed finishing touches of the house remained unfinished. It is almost a trademark of his that he did not finish his buildings.

---

[36] Ibid P234
[37] Ibid p178
[38] Ibid P184

Casa Milá (1906-1910)

Chapter Two- Friedensreich Hundertwasser (1928-2000)

2.1-An overview of Hundertwasser's life and career

Friedrich Stowasser (Friedensreich Hundertwasser) was born in Vienna on 15 December 1928. At the age of five he began to express himself through art. Three years later he was enrolled in Montessori school. He recalled that at Montessori school:

"We were treated individually. They watched each of us to see whether we played with puppets or engines or whatever. Me, I painted"[39].

He developed a love for collecting stamps which stayed with him throughout his life and contributed to his artistic thinking.

"I loved postage stamps long before I became a painter. It was a great joy to collect these little coloured pictures"[40], "It would be impossible to fill a building with fine details like a stamp. Every size has its own law"[41].

Once he learned the rudimentary principals of turning observation into design, organising and other basic skills, school held little interest for him. Also as a child, Hundertwasser was once given small religious votive pictures in church, one of which displayed a painting of a black Madonna with a child and this is the earliest work he recalls affecting

---

[39] Hundertwasser, Harry Rand, 1991 Benedikt Taschen, Verlag P.8
[40] Ibid 160
[41] Ibid 161

him[42]. He briefly attended the Vienna Academy of Fine Arts for three months in 1948 and began producing his works in the late 1940s.[43] Throughout his life, he immersed himself in printing techniques, and doing graphics in colours using metallic imprints.

Tears of an artist (1974)

Hundertwasser spent the first half of 1951 in Morocco and Tunisia; he was impressed by Arabic music and paintings. His first one man show was in February 1952, at the Art Club in Vienna and his first exhibition in Paris was two years later. While living in Japan in 1961, Hundertwasser became interested in the way the Japanese use different names for each stage of their lives depending on general condition, professional status and even mood. Hundertwasser adapted this and changed his name from Friedrich to Friederich and finally to Friedensreich.

He believed:

"If you keep the name you are given, you are a coward, you are not able to be yourself. Then you always do what society or your family has prepared for you. You will never step out of line; you will never be an independent personality"[44].

---

[42] Ibid 12

[43] http://www1.kunsthauswien.com/english/biographie.htm (04/12/2006)

[44] Hundertwasser, Harry Rand, 1991 Benedikt Taschen, Verlag P.18

This rational and flamboyant artist named his single masted ship *"Regentag"* and fulfilled his boyhood dream of long-distance travel; he frequently referred to himself as *"Mr Regentagt"* or *"Captain Regentag"*[45], thus his full name became Friedensreich (rich in peace), Hundertwasser (hundred waters), Regentag (rainy day)[46]. All of these names, in any combination may appear on his work. At a later stage Hundertwasser also added *"Dunkelbunt"*, to his name, which means dark-colourful[47].

Travel and foreign experiences were vital for Hundertwasser. He also spent some time living and absorbing life in Paris. There he enjoyed visiting galleries and, like many artists, took part in discussions which shaped his values and artistic outlook.

Two clouds raining seven colours(1976)

He also spent some time in Sicily, Vienna and North Africa. In 1973 he travelled to the Cape Islands and New Zealand. Because of his love of travel Hundertwasser was exposed to some of the most important and advanced European thinking on art:

"One man has one name; when he has many names he is many persons. That is very good. I have many names and am many persons. I am a painter, an architect, an ecologist"[48].

In addition he had an innate love for nature:

"I see water as a sort of refuge, an escape to which I can always resort"[49].

---

[45] Ibid 17
[46] Ibid 17
[47] Ibid 17
[48] Ibid 17

He was a sensualist and avoided theory, preferring the realm of the senses that never betrayed his own belief about nature. He used the sheer force of contrast and the lush opulence of fierce colours; "*A colourful world is always a synonym for paradise*"[50]to portray incongruous and unusual creations.

His work has been used for flags, stamps, posters, coins, apartment buildings, hotels and even petrol stations. His most famous flag is the Koru flag, symbolising nature's organic power. The Koru flag was a gift to New Zealand in 1983 in appreciation of becoming a New Zealand citizen. The design of the flag intended to represents a combination of past heritage and future hope and the indigenous curling fern exemplifies humanity's harmonious peace with nature.

He has also designed stamps for the Cape Verde islands and the United Nations post administration in Geneva on the occasion of the 35th anniversary of the Universal Declaration of Human Rights[51]. In 1984, he received a gold medal for this beautiful postage stamp from Italy's president Sandro Pertini[52]

---

[49] Ibid 17
[50] Ibid 130
[51] http://en.wikipedia.org/w/index.php?title=Friedensreich_Hundertwasser&oldid=8121 (14/10/2006)
[52] http://www1.kunsthauswien.com/english/biographie.htm (04/12/2006)

"Homo Humus Humanitas".

United Nations 1983: 35th Anniversary of the Universal Declaration of Human Rights

Koru Flag   Cape Verde Stamp

Hundertwasser adopted New Zealand as his official home and regardless of where he went in the world his watch was always set to New Zealand time. When he died in 2000, he returned to his adopted home for the final time, to be buried:

"New Zealand has always been my dream"… "My mother told me that the country there is beautiful, the people are very pleasant and there are no wars"[53].

---

[53] Ao Tea Road: Insel der verlorenen Wünsche, Hamburg:Knaus,1997

2.2- Hundertwasser's theories and ideologies

"The individual's desire to build something should not be deterred"[54]

Hundertwasser's artistic vision expressed itself primarily through philosophy and environmentalism:

"Art is always changing, it must be creative"[55].

In his youth he visualised buildings as violent destroyers of habitat and human scale and his hope for harmony between nature and man took the form of imagined architecture[56]. He often referred to three skins we possess: skin, clothing and architecture.

The main theme in his works is rejection of the straight line:

"The horizontal belongs to nature, the vertical to man"[57]

"Just carrying a ruler with you in your pocket should be forbidden, at least on a moral basis. The ruler is the symptom of the new disease, disintegration of our civilisation"[58]

'Hundertwasser's Dream'

However, bright colours, strong individualism and a reconciliation of humans with nature were also extremely important to Hundertwasser. He believed that ruled straight lines are unhealthy and make people sick as they don't occur in nature:

---

[54] http://www1.kunsthauswein.com/english/gegen-arch.htm (04/12/2006)
[55] Hundertwasser, Harry Rand, 1991 Benedikt Taschen, Verlag P. 15
[56] Ibid 150
[57] Ibid 152
[58] http://www1.kunsthauswein.com/english/gegen-arch.htm (04/12/2006)

"The straight line is a man-made danger. There are so many lines, millions of lines, but only one of them is deadly and that is the straight line drawn with a ruler"[59].
"Functional architecture has proved to be the wrong road to take, similar to painting with a straight- edged ruler"[60]
"The straight line is not a creative line; it is a duplicating line, an imitating line"[61]

Hundertwasser believed that houses consist of windows rather than walls:
"Some people say houses consist of walls. I say houses consist of windows".
"Each individual window has its own right to life"[62]

Street for Survivors (1971)

"For the repetition of identical windows next to each other as in a grid system is a characteristic of concentration camps"[63]

---

[59] Hundertwasser, Harry Rand, 1991 Benedikt Taschen, Verlag P. 45
[60] http://www1.kunsthauswein.com/english/gegen-arch.htm (04/12/2006)
[61] Ibid
[62] http://www1.kunsthauswien.com/english/fenster.htm (04/12/2006)
[63] Ibid

Hundertwasser believed that within each of us is a compilation of memories, sensations, images, dreams and wishes, which he called "Individualism". In his opinion the role of art is to bring this material to a conscious level.[64] He also believed in low cost mass production. His theory of *"Off the shelf technology"* meant that all pre-existing elements should be combined and applied in a novel way in order to reduce costs. [65]

Hundertwasser did not use one specific style for his architecture but a wide variety of styles. He remarked that his state of mind while working was absorption akin to dreaming:

"Once the dream is over, I can't remember what I've dreamt. But the picture remains. The picture is the harvest of the dream"[66].

He strived to make his art rich in effects and animate the colours:
"Colourfulness, variety and diversity are by all means better than the grey, the average grey"[67]

He would have never preached "less is more", and wanted the people of the next generation to see his paintings as an incentive for a creative world:

"Painting is only an exercise towards that aim-a kind of prayer"[68].
"My painting is, I believe, entirely different because it is vegetative painting"[69]

Hundertwasser believed that everybody can have Paradise on earth:
"Paradise is here, only we destroy it"

---

[64] http://hs.riverdale.k12.or.us/~dthompso/art/100h2o/
[65] Hundertwasser, Harry Rand, 1991 Benedikt Taschen, Verlag P.213
[66] Ibid P.135
[67] www1.kunsthauswein.com/English/malerei.htm
[68] Hundertwasser, Harry Rand, 1991 Benedikt Taschen, Verlag P. 134
[69] www1.kunsthauswein.com/English/malerei.htm

Colourfulness, variety and diversity are by all means better than the grey, the average grey "[70].

Flooded sleep 1976

He called his theory of art "transautomatism", based on Surrealist automatism, which is spontaneous writing, drawing, or the like, practiced without conscious aesthetic or moral self-censorship. His first exhibition in Paris at Studio Paul Facchetti developed the theory of *"transautomatism"* [71]. After time, this theory expanded and became known as "The Grammar of Seeing"[72].

"We are already witnessing the miracle of transautomatism…Since we do not yet have total uninhabitability being us, as we are unfortunately not yet in the transautomatism of architecture, we must first achieve total uninhabitability" [73]

[70] http://www1.kunsthauswein.com/english/malerei.htm p.1 (04/12/2006)
[71] http://www1.kunsthauswien.com/english/biographie.htm (04/12/2006)
[72] Hundertwasser, Harry Rand, 1991 Benedikt Taschen, Verlag P. 66
[73] http://www1.kunsthauswein.com/english/gegen-arch.htm (04/12/2006)

Hundertwasser always used the same mechanism for painting; he started from the edge of the sheet and worked towards the centre:

"I cannot paint directly on the canvas without any lines. A clean surface frightens me so I make it dirty somehow"[74].

He explained how he escaped reality through painting:

"For me pictures are gateways through which I can burst into a world which is at once very close to us and very distant…We are inside it, we are imprisoned in it, and yet some inexplicable power denies it to us"[75]

He also constructed his paintings in humble and solitary settings, away from the disruption of people:

"Paintings should be shown as if they were jewels"[76].

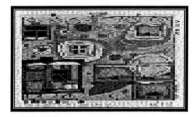

From 'The joy of man' portfolio

For him, painting was a religious activity which guides your hand:

"I think that painting is a religious activity, that then the actual stimulus comes from outside, from something we do not know, an indefinable power"[77]

[74] Hundertwasser, Harry Rand, 1991 Benedikt Taschen, Verlag P. 74
[75] Ibid 36
[76] Ibid 84
[77] http://www1.kunsthauswein.com/english/malerei.htm p.2 (04/12/2006)

Hundertwasser was also a firm believer in ecology:

"Ecology means nature and the cycle of nature, but one important factor is left out by the ecologists, and that is the feeling of being creative. Without creation and creativity, nothing works, especially not in ecology"[78].

He was also well known for his performance art. He appeared naked in public in an effort to promote an ecologically friendly flush-less toilet[79] and also took part in nude demonstrations in Munich and Vienna against architecture's inhumane environment. He believed that architecture should not be called art and declared that the design of any building should be influenced by the aesthetics of its eventual tenants.

2.3- Hundertwasser's Influences.

The earlier work (Nierenstein Collection)[80] of fellow Austrian artist, Egon Schiele, which he first encountered in 1948 at an exhibition in Vienna commemorating Schiele's death, made a considerable impact on Hundertwasser.

Hundertwasser appreciated Schiele's expression of peaceful beauty and glimpses of another world and was deeply impressed by the colours he used:

"For me the houses of Schiele were living beings. For the first time I felt that the outside walls were skins. He painted them as if there were no difference between the skin of a naked girl and the skin of a house"[81]. *"I would like to be estimated as Klimt and Schiele, as an innovator in the history of art"*[82].

---

[78] Hundertwasser, Harry Rand, 1991 Benedikt Taschen, Verlag P. 74
[79] http://en.wikipedia.org/w/index.php?title=Friedensreich_Hundertwasser&oldid=8121 (14/10/2006)
[80] Hundertwasser, Harry Rand, 1991 Benedikt Taschen, Verlag P. 13
[81] Ibid 14
[82] Ibid 131

One of the main influences behind the creations of Hundertwasser is the works of the important Spanish architect, Antonio Gaudí. Hundertwasser's architectural work is comparable to Antonio Gaudí in its biomorphic forms and in the use of tile. Hundertwasser himself was aware of his similarity and declared of one of his projects: *"My building will have something of Gaudi"[83]*.

Hundertwasser created a vertical village for the city of Vienna under special request, which depicts his ideals and reflects the inspiration of Gaudí. This vertical village sometimes called *"The Löwengasse structure"*, more often known as the Hundertwasserhaus consists of renewable and colourful plaster on the walls with a vaulting joyous roofline which evokes Gaudí's "Casa Mila". As in Gaudí's "Park Güell", this building has opulent stairs leading to the street and there are great curving parabolic entry arches. Hundertwasser has tinted the concrete in order to eliminate weather erosion and has elaborated the façade by using silver tiles.

---

[83] Ibid 210

2.4- Some of Hundertwasser's most popular works

Hundertwasser was a dedicated craftsman, architect and artist for forty years and earned worldwide recognition and international respect as one of the world's greatest artists. Although Hundertwasser is well known for his boldly coloured rare and precious paintings, he is more widely renowned for his irregular architectural designs. The style and originality of his works almost have a quality of magic in them. None of the locks, doorknobs, windows or doors are the same in any of his buildings, which evokes a sense of unique individualism and creativity. Most of his imaginative works are characterised by land, sea and sky.

The **Hundertwasser House /Hundertwasserhaus Wien (1977-1986)**, is Hundertwasser's most popular work. The apartment house is located in Vienna, Austria. The construction of this apartment block, which was funded by the Austrian government, began in 1977 and was completed in 1986. It was inhabited by its first tenants in 1986.[84] This assymetrical house features undulating floors, a roof covered with earth and grass, and large trees growing from inside the rooms. This unique masterpiece boasts winding corridors, uneven floors, natural curves, playful angles and decorative elements with a non-sensical layout scheme to the apartments.

Hundertwasser took no payment for the design of this house, as he wanted to prevent something ugly from going up in its place. Hundertwasser's goal was to make cities more harmonious places in which to live. He claimed buildings should be semi-submerged under undulating meadows, and that floors and pavements should be uneven to better resemble forest paths. Most of his buildings are characterized with generous helpings of green trees, grass and bushes, one way to bring the inhabitants closer to nature:

---

[84] http://www.escapeartist.com/OREQ16/Vienna.html (15/02/2007)

'Man is shielded from nature by three levels of insulation: cities, houses and clothes. " [85]

Hundertwasser tried to limit the effect of the first two through his architecture; as for the third, he was known to occasionally run round his buildings naked. The Hundertwasserhaus was turned over to the tenants on 17 February 1986, when 70,000 visitors attended the "Open House".

Within the house there are 50 apartments, four offices, 16 private terraces and three communal terraces, and a total of 250 trees. The Hundertwasserhaus is one of Austria's most visited buildings, and has become part of Austria's cultural heritage.

Hundertwasserhaus Wien, Vienna (1977-1986)

"The windows are an equivalent of the eyes", (Hundertwasser, April 1991). [86]

---

[85] http://www.lonelyplanet.com/theme/art/art_friedensreich.htm
[86] (Hundertwasser, 1991), http://www1.kunsthauswien.com/english/haut.htm

Hundertwasserhaus Wien (1977-1986)

A famous stamp called *Cept Europalia* depicts the Hundertwasser House. This stamp appeared in Austria in March 1987.[87]

---

[87] http://www1.kunsthauswien.com/english/biographie.htm (04/12/2006)

'Blue Blues'
Austria 2000. Hundertwasser in Memoriam

Chapter three- Similarities between Gaudí's and Hundertwasser's works

3.1-Gaudí's influence on Hundertwasser

Antoni Gaudí's work has been categorized as Art Nouveau architecture, a precursor to modern architecture. His style was later echoed by that of Austrian architect Friedensreich Hundertwasser (1928–2000). Hundertwasser's work can be described as hypnotic and it shows an almost obsessive preoccupation with spiral forms. Buildings, landscapes and human forms are all transformed into abstract dynamic spirals. His colouring shows Asian and Persian influence, concentrating on gold and silver and especially phosphorescent red and green. The majority of the works of both Hundertwasser and Gaudí boasts individuality.

The Spiral Tree, Hundertwasser, (1975)

Hundertwasser's individuality also shows evidence of Gaudí's influence. This is most obvious in Hundertwasser's inclusion of irregular almost incidental forms in his building design. Hundertwasser expresses an antipathy to severity and austerity in architecture which he sees in the use of straight lines. Some of Hundertwasser's favourite forms of architecture are found in slums, where inhabitants built their homes out of any materials they could find:

"Everyone should make his own architecture; he should be able to construct what he likes, with features, grass or paper, even if the building collapses"[88].

3.2-Similarities in style and technique

There are striking similarities between the work of Gaudí and that of Hundertwasser in biomorphic forms and especially in their use of light, additional windows, natural curves and gardens. Instead of relying on geometric shapes, both architects expressed their love for nature and mimicked the way trees and humans grow and stand upright. The hyperboloids and paraboloids in the arches of many of Gaudí's buildings were borrowed from nature and reinforced by steel rods, allowing their designs to resemble elements of the enviornment. The love for nature is clearly inevitable in some of their most popular works. Gaudí's work was greatly influenced by forms of nature and this is reflected by the use of curved construction stones, twisted iron sculptures, and organic-like forms which are traits of Gaudí's Barcelona architecture. The combination of original design, interesting shaped stonework, and vibrant colours in both architect's work provide a truly breathtaking visual experience.

3.2a- Love of nature

The love for nature is clearly evident in Gaudí's apartment building Casa Milá and Hundertwasser's Hundertwasserhaus in Vienna. Casa Milá represents the clearest assertion of Gaudí's mature organic style. The unprecedented absence of straight lines and evocation of nature is one of the most explored aspects of his architectural identity. The cave- like articulation of windows and interior spaced also betray a scientific tone. Casa Milá is actually two buildings, each arranged around a curvilinear central patio, and

---

[88] Hundertwasser Chipp, Herschel B. and Brenda Richardson ,1986

each with a separate entrance.[89] The façade is composed of large blocks of stone, from garraf on the lower floors and vilafranca on the floors above. Thanks to a framework of pillars and steel girders, Gaudí was able to eliminate bearing walls. The façade has three differentiated parts: The six floors are marked by sinuous arrangement of stone blocks. The two-level is distinguished from the body of the building by different changes in materials and colour. The attic façade is made of smooth, white stones. When Gaudí died in 1926, all traces of his work were erased from the Milas private apartments on the first floor as Mila's wife, Roser Segimon, had taken an intense dislike to Gaudí and decided to decorate in the style of Louis XVI. When the Caixa de Catalunya Savings Bank acquired the building, details of ceilings were rediscovered and were made available to view by the public.[90]

In 1961, Casa Milá was included in the Barcelona City Halls catalogue of monuments; in 1969, it was declared a national monument; and in 1984, it was included by UNESCO in a World Art Heritage list.[91] The roof of Casa Milá sports an imitation of the tile curved bench in Güell Park and a humorous landscape of shrubs and trees.

Nature was extremely significant in Hundertwasser's work also:
"Paradises can only be made with our own hands, with our own creativity in harmony with the free creativity of nature", (Hundertwasser, April, 1991).[92]

"Art must meet man's and nature's pace.
Art must respect nature and the laws of nature.
Art must respect man and man's inspiration for true and durable values.
Art must again be a bridge between the creativity of nature and the creativity of man.

---

[89] Gaudí of Barcelona, Lluis Permanyer, 1997 p. 156

[90] Gaudí of Barcelona, Lluis Permanyer, 1997 p .164
[91] Ibid p.166
[92] Antoni Gaudí, Judith Carmel-Arthur, Carlton, 1999 p.16

41

Art must regain its universal function for all and not be just a fashionable business for insiders.

Art must free itself from the ties of guided intellectual tutorship.
Art should not suffer speculation and cultural industrialization.
Art should not endure dogmatic enslavement through negative theories.
Art must have a purpose.
Art must create lasting values.
The courage to strive for beauty in harmony with nature". (Hundertwasser, October 1990).[93]

In Hundertwasser's vertical village, "The Löwengasse structure", stands the famous Hundertwasserhaus, which consists of renewable and colourful plaster on the walls with a vaulting joyous roofline that evokes Gaudí's Casa Milá. In the Hundertwasserhaus, the roof is covered with earth, grass, and large trees growing from inside the rooms and follows a similar pattern as Casa Milá with its winding corridors, uneven floors and decorative elements with a non-sensical layout scheme to the apartments. Each of the apartments has access to a small piece of nature in the form of roof gardens. The gardens have nearly two hundred and fifty trees and a large grass lawn.[94]

Nothing in either building is uniform and the ground plans for each floor are completely different. Also, another main characteristic that is evident in the works of both architects is their ability to create unusual, childish creations usually connected to nature. Both architects betray a symbiosis between architecture and nature that marks their eclectic style. Hundertwasser's revolutionary architectural ideas include topping buildings with trees and areas where animals can graze, and creating uneven floor surfaces, likewise in Gaudí's work.

"It is good to walk on uneven floors and regain our human balance",

---

[93] Ibid
[94] http://www.travel.dk.com/vienna/dk/highlight/hundertwasserhaus

(Hundertwasser, April, 1991).[95]

The Rogner Bad Blumau spa resort in Austria is also a definite expression of Hundertwasser's love for nature. The contribution of various architectural forms, where roofs are made of grass, and the windows face forest courtyards is also an indication of how he transformed the environment he worked on, as did Gaudí.

Casa Milá (1906-1910)

[95] http://www1.kunsthauswien.com/english/boden.htm

3.2b- Tiling:

The Rogner Bad Blumau spa also shows how important the use of tile was to Hundertwasser. Hundertwasser shares some of the same ideologies as Gaudí, as his preference was to decorate surfaces with basic everyday materials such as coloured tiles (Aragonese trencadís technique) and cheap stone.[96] Gaudí's use of tiles is clearly evident on the curved benches in his Parc Güell, a Municipal Park in Barcelona. An expressive and cosmopolitan use of polychrome ceramic tiling became one of Gaudí's stylistic trademarks.

Parc Güell, built 1900-1914 is a landscape of extravagance nestled in the hills above Barcelona. This extensive park was to accommodate as many as sixty middle class households in a walled community, complete with a play area, market and plaza. Only two houses were built and the church that was planned to symbolically arise from the hill was never constructed. Parc Güell reveals Gaudí's unprecedented fusion of colour, natural and artificial space and structural form. There is a visible alliance with nature in repeated motifs of animals, plants, rocks and caves complemented by arbitrary mosaic patterns which adorn the parks undulating structures. The polychromatic, tiled parapet-bench which effortlessly curls around the flat roof of the market hall is amongst the most famous examples of Gaudí's use of ceramic, porcelain and glass shards. Immediately beyond the entrance gates a sinuous split staircase climbs up through the terraces of the park. On either side of the balustrades, which are covered in white ceramic fragments, rise curved crenulated walls decorated in a chequerboard pattern of tiles.

A triangular garden and fountain divides the stairs at the base. The unfinished Parc Güell is a true masterpiece.[97]

---

[96] Antoni Gaudi: The complete buildings, Rainer Zerbst, Taschen, 2002p.75

[97] The lesson of Gaudí, Carlos Flores, Espasa, 2002p.254

Hundertwasser's Rogner Bad Blumau spa resort echo the same ideology in tiling. At Rogner-Bad Blumau, an odd and extraordinary hotel and spa in the remote Austrian countryside there are terra-cotta floors that sway and curl. The pillars at the entrance are gold, white, bright red, royal blue and mauve. The outside walls are black and white with uneven tiles and the windows are painted yellow, red and white. There are chequered designs over the doorways. The entrance is an arrangement of bold coloured tiles, giving a wavy effect. Doors and windows are painted in an array of colours, and the façades are decorated elaborately with mosaics. On the roof of the building, there are green areas, where chestnut, beech and lilacs trees grow. Guest rooms are in buildings whose shapes suggest recumbent dinosaurs. Swooping rooftops are covered with grass and trees; they dip to the ground like branches heavy with snow. Windows are placed haphazardly, rectangles, circles and squares, frames painted in natural colors and neon tints. These design factors accumulate to make an architectural statement so unusual and at the same time also relate to the similarities in Gaudí's works. An expressive and cosmopolitan use of polychrome ceramic tiling became a favorite stylistic trademark of both Gaudí and Hundertwasser along with a consistently strong emphasis on materials in their work.[98]

---

[98] Park Güell, Gaudi's Utopia, Joseph M. Carandellp.87

45

Rogner-Bad Blumau, Hotel and Spa (1993-1997)

Bench, Parc Güell (1900-1914

Hundertwasserhaus Wien, Vienna (1977-1986)

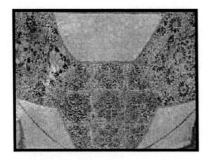

Parc Güell (1900-1914)

3.3-La SagradaFamília and Church of St. Barbara

Both architects have been involved in the construction of churches during their lifetime. Gaudí was commissioned to build what is now known as one of Barcelona's most famous landmarks, La SagradaFamília, which remains incomplete.

While on a much smaller scale, Hundertwasser accepted the task of redesigning the Church of Santa Barbara in Bärnbach, Austria.

La SagradaFamília (1883-1926) (The Sacred Family)

Gaudí's church in Barcelona remains inflected towards the neo gothic idiomas of his early career only in its emphatic height and ideological purpose. The building is meant to harbour five naves and the choir galleries could ideally accommodate 1500 vocalists and approximately seven pipe organs.[99] There are figural sculptures depicting biblical scenes. In addition to architectural, symbolic and metaphorical imagery, Gaudí also adapted textual inscriptions to the fabric of the building. In doing so, he identified the cathedral entity as an amalgamation of text and image. Parabolic arches and towers are one of Gaudí's most famous trademarks. The earliest of these sketches was for a church and

---

[99] Antoni Gaudí, Judith Carmel-Arthur, Carlton, 1999 p.16

monastery for the Franciscans of Tangier (1892-1993), and reveals the beginnings of Gaudí's ideas for the cluster of parabolic towers used subsequently in La SagradaFamilia. The first appearance of parabolic arches is in the Palau Güell (1887-1991), and the Colegio Teresiano, Barcelona (1889-1994). [100]

While working on the mature phases for the SagradaFamilia, Gaudí was simultaneously engaged on another important commission for sacred structures: the unrealized Chapel and incomplete Crypt (1898-1917) of the Güell Colony in Sant Coloma de Cervelló. Gaudí planned a small Chapel for Park Güell, which is only the second church of Gaudí's career. [101] The exquisite craftsmanship of the brick and the sophisticated arrangement of polychrome, ceramic surfaces reflects Gaudí's gift as a structural engineer. The church betrays symbiosis between architecture and nature that marks Gaudí's eclectic style. His favouring of nature as the fundamental frame of reference for the innovation of both symbolism and structure is extreme, while his use and expression of raw materials divorces his work from superficial, populist expressions of Art Noveau.
The exteriors of Gaudí's buildings are thoroughly indicative of his mannered interpretation of the Mudèjar style. A Mudèjar inflection is also seen in Gaudí's proclivity towards dense surface ornamental and patterning, created by the horizontal detailing of decorative brickwork and polychrome, ceramic cladding.

Hundertwasser just built one church. In 1984 Hundertwasser accepted the task of redesigning the Church of Santa Barbara in Bärnbach in Austria. Although this is a small scale church in comparison to La SagradaFamília, they have similar characteristics. Hundertwasser's church has twelve gates, standing for all the great religions in the world; in comparison with La SagradaFamília which envisaged twelve bell-towers, four for each façade, each tower is being dedicated to an apostle. Hundertwasser designed the aureole behind the altar, the floor of the presbyterium and the spiral of the window behind the

---

[100] Ibid p.18
[101] Ibid p. 19

48

baptismal font.[102] Both churches are extremely ornate and depict biblical images. Hundertwasser sees the church as *"a bridge to nature and as a creation of God"[103]*, likewise with La SagradaFamília to which Gaudí devoted the latter part of his life

La SagradaFamília (1883-1926), Barcelona

Church of St. Barbara, Bärnbach 1984-1988

---

[102] www1.kunsthauswien.com/English/st-barbara.htm
[103] www.baernbach.at/Tourismus/Kirche_kirche.htm

49

Conclusion

Antoni Gaudí and Friedensreich Hundertwasser were gifted architects of their time. The combination of skill and individualism contributed to their world famous masterly architectural designs, which are now recognised as some of the most famous landmarks in Europe. Equally important is the fact that both men had similar interests. They both shared a love for nature, a hatred of straight lines, a strong belief in the use of tiling and a love for bold, vivid colours.

The buildings of Gaudí and Hundertwasser are enchanting with their incongruous, childish colours and shapes. The disorderly arrangement of tiles and raw materials provide amusement and are a source of inspiration. The famous works of Gaudí and Hundertwasser transcend normality and never cease to amaze the eye, and the imagination.

It was Gaudí, however who began this architectural experiment. His death came when Hundertwasser was two years of age, and it is Gaudí's philosophy which had a significant impact on Hundertwasser, a fact which is clearly reflected in the Austrian architect's most famous architectural buildings.

Antoni Gaudí has always been of great importance for the cultural development of Europe. Gaudí, in Spain, and Hundertwasser, in Austria, have played a key role in this development. Gaudí's impact and influence on Hundertwasser has been of enormous significance. Together their creativity, imagination and similarities have had a profound effect on European art and our common European heritage.

Bibliography

Secondary Sources:

Books:

- Artigas, Isabel, *Gaudi, Complete Works,* Taschen, 2007

- Bergos, Masso Juan, *The Man and his work,* Brown and company, 1999

- Burry Mark, *Expiatory Church of the Sagrada Familia,* Phaidon Press, 1999

- Cirlot, Juan- Eduardo, *Gaudi: An introduction to his architecture,* Triangle press, 2000

- Crippa, Maria Antoietta, *Antoni Gaudi,* Taschen, 2003

- Crippa, Maria Antoietta, *The architect's complete Vision,* Rizzoli Int. Publications, 2002

- Gaudi, Antoni, *Obra Completa,* H.K Ediciones, 2002

- Harel, Joham, *Hundertwasser KunstHausWien,* Taschen, 1999

- Schediwy, Robert, *Hundertwasser Häuser- Dokumente einer Kontroverse über zeitgemässe Architektur,* Editon Tusch, 1999

- Koschatzky, Walter, *Friedensreich Hundertwasser: The complete Graphic work,* Alan Wofsy fine arts, 1986

- Lahuerta, Juan José, *Antoni Gaudi 1852-1926,* Deutsche Verlags Anstalt, 2003

- Muthesius, Angelika, *Hundertwasser's Architecture: Building for nature and humankind,* Taschen, 1997

- Permayer, Lluis, *Gaudi of Barcelona,* Rizzoli Int. Publications, 1997

- Rand, Harry, *Hundertwasser,* Taschen, 1991

- Reistany, Pierre, *Hundertwasser: The painter with five skins,* Taschen, 1998

- Roe, Jeremy, *Gaudi: Architect and Artist,* Parkstone Press ltd., 2006

- Sterner, Gabriele, *Antoni Gaudi: Architecture in Barcelona,* Barrons educational series Inc., 1985

- Thiebaut, Philippe, *Gaudi: Visionary Architect,* Harry N. Abrams Inc., 2002

- Varnedoe, Kirk, *Vienna 1900: Art, Architecture, Design,* Museum of Modern Art, 1986

- Wang, Wilfried, *Contemporary Architecture in Germany 1970-1996: 50 Buildings,* Birkhauser Verlag, 1997

- Zerbest, Rainer, *Antoni Gaudi,* Taschen, 2002

Internet Sites:

www.cervantes.es accessed on: 19/10/06

www.barcelonagallery.com accessed on: 23/10/06

www.antonigaudi.com accessed on: 15/11/06

www.kunsthauswein.com accessed on: 3/2/07

www.baernbach.at/Tourismus/Kirche_kirche.htmaccessed on: 12/12/06

www.puckergallery.com/hundertwasser.html accessed on: 06/9/06

www.taschen.com/pages/en/catalogue/series/portfolios/all/facts/23504.htm accessed on:
02/3/07

www.grasshut.co accessed on: 22/5/07

http://www.escapeartist.com/OREQ16/Vienna.html accessed on: 12/9/06

http://www1.kunsthauswien.com/english/biographie.htm accessed on: 04/11/06

www.badblumau.com accessed on: 19/9/06

http://liong-faye.org.nz/koru-flag/ accessed on: 08/2/07

http://www.vrvienna.com/iview_quicktime/source/hundert_wasser_haus.html accessed
on: 25/1/07

http://www.lonelyplanet.com/theme/art/art_friedensreich.htm accessed on: 22/04/07

http://www.darmstadt.de/en/sights/hundertwasser/index.html accessed on: 12/09/06

http://hs.riverdale.k12.or.us/~dthompso/art/100h2o/ accessed on: 02/10/06

http://www.baernbach.at/Tourismus/Kirche_Hundertwasser.htm accessed on: 14/12/06

www.art-perfect.de/hundertwasserhaus.htm accessed on: 30/04/07